HOW TO CREATE A COMMUNITY

Step-by-step guide

LUCIA BUSTAMANTE

For Marco, Marta, Ernesto, Melisa and Luna.

Contents

I. Introduction

Why this book? 11

About the author 15

II. Community as a Concept

What is a Community? 20

Online vs. Offline 22

Why do people vibrate better in Community? 25

III. Building a Community

Why do you, your company, or the world need a Community? 30

Mission and Vision 32

Defining the profile of the followers 35

What does the Community offer its members? 42

How to involve Community members 44

Incorporation of new members: Onboarding 46

The team behind (and in front) of the Community 49

Identify stakeholders 51

Identify the right platform 54

IV. The Future

Planning is key 60

How do you maintain a Community? Does it "end" at some point? 62

Metrics to measure Community growth 63

V. Case Study: Mujeres IT 67

VI. Checklist 75

VII. Community Planner 79

I. Introduction

Why this book?

This book does not focus on the competitive advantages that a community has for a business, but on the keys and steps to create a community of any type and non-profit, founded on a need or a common objective of a sector of the society.

I have always liked connecting with people and connecting people. Unintentionally, I had adopted the habit or ability to generate communities, to bring individuals together around a theme, or a cause that moved my heart, as it was in the past, making visible the art of emerging artists within the "Colectivo.uy" community, or connecting local freelancers in "Freelo", or my most significant driving force and the one that has led me to create a community with more than 1,000 members, working together to reduce the gender gap in technology in "Mujeres IT".

I have given talks on how to create communities, and I have offered mentoring on this, one repeated factor is not understanding its need. A community is a product. As such it arises to solve a problem, to satisfy a need, to provide enjoyment. So why not think of communities as products? Why not apply design thinking to creating a community? Why not plan a community for the future as a scalable product?

This text is intended to be a reference guide when you are thinking about creating a social space.
This book will ask you the questions you should ask yourself, making you reflect on the present and the future. Because a community is born, lives, and sometimes even dies. But how long does it live? How does it survive?

I have a lot to tell you, and I would like you to finish this reading with an understanding of your current situation, an identification of the future you want to create, and the ability to execute a plan yourself.

I would also like you to be able to teach others what you have learned and what you have applied, and I would even more like you to share the results with me!

About the author

I am Lucia Bustamante, a curious and restless woman. I have an introverted side, which I need to rediscover from time to time, but I also have an extroverted side, which drives me to do things like write this book.

I have computer processing and design training, so I consider myself a hybrid who navigates between the technical and the creative.
In recent years, I have developed a leadership role as a design manager, leading several teams and projects for various industries. I am a mentor, and in that act, I discovered not only a part of myself that I didn't know, one that enjoys motivating others and connecting, but I also discovered a huge source of learning and inspiration for my professional and personal life.

Connecting with people has always been one key to my success. Accept that we do not have superpowers and often need friends, allies, and role models. I have built communities on a different scale, the most recent is Mujeres IT, which today has more than 1000 members, and is a benchmark in Latin America.
In addition, I am a speaker, I am interested in disseminating the practice of

design and talking about the role of women in the industry.

Now that you know me, let's get started.

II. Community as a concept

What is a Community?

A community is a space of interaction in which people can express their opinions and share experiences. Within a community, individuals have various elements in common. These can be sociodemographic, such as territory, age, language, or values.

A community can also be formed from common interests, and these are the reasons why people decide to be part of the community in the first place, and will be what motivates them to stay over time. A community generates a sense of belonging and opens a space for the exchange of experiences, resources, and opinions among its members.

Some key aspects of the community concept:

Interconnection: Communities are made up of individuals who are interconnected in some way, whether through geographic location, common interests, shared identities, or similar goals. These connections can be both physical and virtual in the digital age.

Interdependence: Members of a community depend on each other in some way. They may depend on shared resources, emotional support, collaboration on projects, or simply to meet their basic and social needs.

Shared identity: Communities often have a shared identity or sense of belonging that unites their members. This may be based on characteristics such as culture, religion, professional interests, ethnicity, or shared history.

Active participation: Communities thrive when their members regularly participate in activities and contribute to collective well-being. This participation can take many forms, such as attending events, collaborating on projects, volunteering, or supporting each other in times of need.

Diversity: Although communities often share a common identity, they also tend to be diverse in terms of individual opinions, skills, backgrounds, and experiences. This diversity can enrich the community by offering different perspectives and skills.

Resilience: Strong communities can face challenges and adversity together. Solidarity and mutual support within the community can help overcome obstacles and promote resilience in difficult times.

A community generates a sense of belonging and opens a space for the exchange of experiences, resources, and opinions among its members.

Online vs. Offline

The nature of a community, whether online or offline, depends on several factors that can influence how its members form, interact, and operate.

Some of these factors include:

Access to technology: The availability of technology and Internet access is a key factor in determining whether a community will be online or offline. Online communities typically form when members have access to Internet-connected devices, such as computers, smartphones, or tablets, allowing them to participate in virtual activities and discussions. On the other hand, offline communities can emerge in environments where access to technology is limited or where face-to-face interactions are preferred.

Member interests and needs: Members' interests and needs can influence how a community organizes itself. Online communities can form around specialized interests or specific niches that may not be easily available in the offline world. On the other hand, offline communities can emerge in response to local needs or specific problems that require face-to-face interaction to address.

Geographic location: The geographic location of members can also influence whether a community is online or offline. Offline communities tend to be more focused on a specific geographic area, where members can interact in person at local events, meetings, or activities. In contrast, online communities can bring together members from different parts of the world who share common interests, without being limited by geographic location.

Culture and communication preferences: Cultural differences and members' communication preferences can influence how a community chooses to interact. Some groups prefer in-person communication and interaction, which favors the formation of offline communities. Others may feel more comfortable with online communication and virtual participation, leading to the formation of online communities.

Of course, a community can adopt a hybrid character, in this way it develops online activities, but also encourages direct contact with its members. These communities obtain specific advantages from in-person and virtual reality.

Some examples of communities:

A family

A neighborhood

A camp

A foundation

A religious association

A scientific community

"There is immense power when a group of people with similar interests come together to work toward the same goals."

Idowu Koyenikan

Why do people vibrate better in Community?

The social interaction and sense of belonging that a community provides fulfills the basic need for human connection, and that can be seen in Maslow's Pyramid. The community offers emotional support, mutual understanding, and the opportunity to share experiences and knowledge. Who doesn't like to feel heard and supported?

Additionally, **the diversity of perspectives and skills within a community enriches exchange, fostering continuous learning and personal growth**. Collaboration and teamwork are also more effective in a community setting, as different people can bring their strengths as individuals to achieve shared goals.

Community provides a context in which people can become empowered, feel valued, and contribute meaningfully, promoting greater well-being and life satisfaction.

Maslow's Pyramid

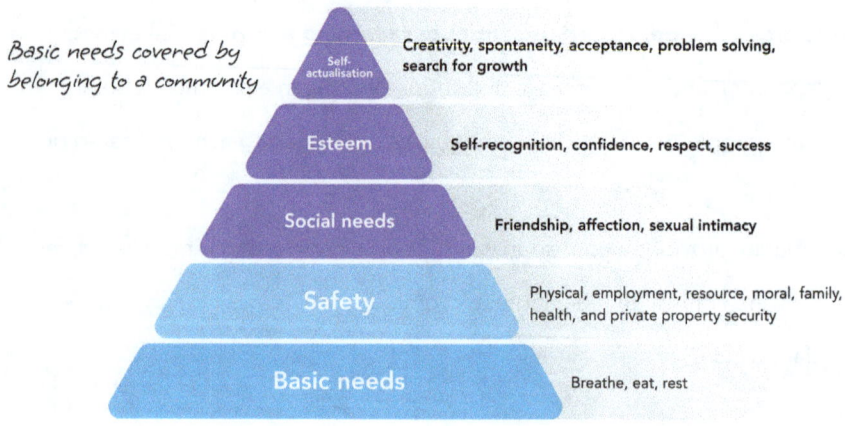

III. Building a Community

Why do you, your company, or the world need a Community?

This is a key question to ask yourself before getting involved in the creation process. Whether you are thinking about creating a community for your business, or as an individual, you have to ask yourself, firstly, what is the need that drives you, and you have to be able to answer this question.

The purpose or reason for being in the community you are going to create will be what defines its mission and its values.

In mentoring sessions, some people, mostly founders, ask me how to build a community for their companies. I start by asking them the aforementioned question, because many times they assume that a community is the best way to approach their audience, and that may not be the case.

I'll tell you an anecdote. One person asked me about the steps to building a community of designers. The product consisted of a website and template development service. This person was convinced that a community could increase the engagement of its users, even increase their number. But why? He didn't know how to answer this question very well. So I proposed to him to redefine his audience and his service, so together we concluded that he did not need a community, but rather a talent pool, in which designers could show their work, to attract clients who wanted to buy their templates.

The door to building a community or adding a social component to that structure was left open, according to how the audience's behavior would be observed.

From there, it would be evaluated whether it would be necessary to generate a space for interaction. Its users share a passion for web design, and that could be a good card to play.

With this story, I want to show you that you should reflect on necessity and purpose. If you have been able to answer the initial question, let's continue.

Mission and Vision

Before shaping your community you must have a defined idea and purpose, and sorry if I insist on this, but it is very important. You must be able to describe the value that the community would bring to society or the target audience. For this, you should already have an idea of whom the community would be aimed at, either an audience you already have, or an audience you want to reach, but we will talk about the target audience in the next chapter.

At this stage, you will think about the community's values that align with your purpose. Once you define those values, think about the mission. Imagine it as the fuel that drives you every day to take the community forward.

The Mission

The mission, or "mission statement," is a concise statement that describes an organization's fundamental purpose, main objectives, and shared values. Also known as a "mission statement," it articulates the organization's reason for being and provides guidance for its activities and strategic decisions.

> The main purpose of a mission statement is to communicate clearly and directly what the organization does, who it does it for, and why it does it. This helps align members and other stakeholders around the organization's shared goals and values.

An effective mission statement is usually **brief, memorable, and easy to understand**, but it also reflects the essence of the organization and its long-term vision. It is an important tool for establishing a distinctive identity and guiding the development of strategies and actions consistent with the organization's fundamental principles.

Mission Statement Example:
"In our community, we work together to create an environment where everyone feels valued, safe, and empowered to reach their full potential. Our mission is to build strong bonds, promote diversity, and celebrate the unique strengths of each individual, as we work toward a more prosperous and united future for all."

The Vision

Your community vision will be a statement that describes **the desired state in the future** toward which you want to move. It is a clear and compelling picture of what the community aspires to achieve over the long term and provides strategic direction and a sense of shared purpose.

Vision typically answers questions such as, "What do we want to achieve?" "What do we want the world to be like in the future?" or "What is our biggest dream or ideal?" It is an inspiring statement that articulates the community's highest goals and fundamental aspirations and serves as a reference point to guide long-term decision-making and action.

An effective vision is **clear, specific, achievable, relevant, and meaningful** to community members. It must be ambitious enough to inspire and motivate, but also practical and realistic to be achievable with effort and commitment. The vision helps align all community members around a common goal and provides a framework for evaluating progress and measuring success over time.

Before shaping your community you must have a defined idea and purpose, and sorry if I insist on this, but it is very important. You must be able to describe the value that the community would bring to society or the target audience.

Defining the profile of the followers

Knowing and defining the profile of your followers is essential for the success and effectiveness of any community initiative, whether on social networks, online groups, non-profit ventures, or any other type of community.

Knowing and defining the profile of a community's followers lies in its ability to enhance the connection and commitment of its members. First, understanding who your followers are allows you to **personalize** content and communications, significantly increasing their likelihood of actively engaging.

This personalization makes the content more relevant and engaging, showing followers they are valued as individuals within the community.

Furthermore, knowledge of the followers' profile facilitates **more effective interaction**. By understanding their interests, concerns and needs, more authentic and meaningful conversations can be generated, strengthening the connection between members and fostering a sense of belonging. This genuine interaction is essential to building strong relationships within the community.

Another key benefit of knowing your followers' profile is the ability to effectively **segment** your audience. This segmentation allows specific messages to be targeted to particular groups within the community, ensuring that each segment receives relevant and useful information. This not only improves the follower experience but also increases the likelihood of positive response and active engagement.

In addition, analyzing the profiles of followers can reveal **growth opportunities** for the community. Identifying areas where the community can expand or diversify, whether by seeking new demographic segments or exploring emerging topics of interest, is essential to its continued evolution and development.

Ultimately, comprehending the identity and motivations of your followers is the key to crafting effective engagement strategies. By tailoring activities, events, and programs to align with the community's interests and needs, you can significantly boost engagement and loyalty. This not only benefits the community in the short term but also paves the way for sustainable and enduring growth.

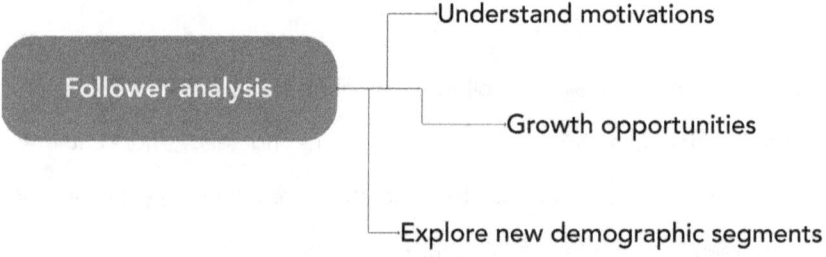

To better visualize your audience, their characteristics, and their needs, I recommend the use of two tools. One is widely used in a product, the well-known Value Proposition Canvas, and the other is widely used by user experience designers: the User Persona. Below, I describe how you can use these tools to benefit your community.

Value Proposition Canvas: unleashing the potential of your community

Understanding and offering value to your members is essential. This is where the Value Proposition Canvas emerges as a powerful tool, offering a structured approach to creating compelling value propositions **tailored to your needs** and wants. It is very useful to visualize if there is a connection and coherence between what you propose and the needs of potential members.
The tool provides a framework for identifying the specific benefits and features that resonate most strongly with your audience.

Let's see how leveraging this tool can elevate your community-building efforts to new heights:

Deep understanding of member needs: The Value Proposition Canvas prompts you to dive deep into the wants, needs, and pain points of your community members. By empathizing with their experiences and challenges, you gain invaluable insights that lay the foundation for creating cohesive offerings.

Clarity in value delivery: Building a successful community depends on delivering tangible value to its members. The Value Proposition Canvas helps distill the key benefits and solutions your community provides, ensuring clarity in your message. This clarity fosters trust and engagement among members, driving long-term retention and advocacy.

Aligning services with member preferences: Armed with a deep understanding of member needs, the Value Proposition Canvas allows you to tailor your offers to perfectly align with their preferences. Whether it's educational resources, networking opportunities, or exclusive benefits, you can adjust your offerings to deliver maximum value and relevance.

Iterative improvement and innovation: Community dynamics are constantly evolving, requiring a flexible and iterative approach to value creation. The Value Proposition Canvas allows you to continually refine and improve your offerings based on real-time feedback and changing member needs. This agility ensures that your community remains vibrant and responsive to changing trends and preferences.

Differentiation and competitive advantage: In a saturated landscape, differentiation is key to standing out and attracting members to your community. By leveraging the Value Proposition Canvas to articulate unique value propositions, you establish a distinctive identity that differentiates your community from the competition. This differentiation not only attracts new members but also fosters a sense of belonging and loyalty among existing ones.

The Value Proposition Canvas has the following format:

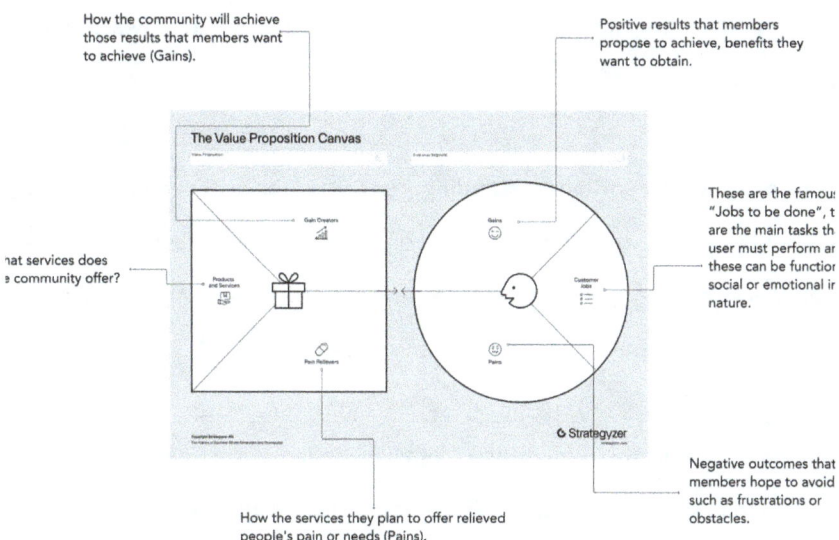

You can continually refine and improve your services based on real-time feedback and changing member needs.

User Persona

This tool is considered a piece of research and is exceptionally useful when defining a community's audience. Here I explain why:

Creating detailed profiles: User Personas allow you to create detailed profiles of the different types of potential community members. These profiles include demographic information, behaviors, interests, needs, and goals for each type of user, providing a complete understanding of who they are and what they are looking for.

Identification of needs and desires: When developing User Personas, a deep research process is carried out to identify the needs, wants, challenges, and pain points of the target audience. This helps understand what motivates potential members to join the community and what kind of value they are looking for.

Focus on empathy and understanding: User Personas foster an empathetic mindset by putting yourself in the shoes of different audience segments. This deeper understanding helps create a community that is more inclusive and responsive to members' diverse needs and experiences.

Personalization of the experience: With well-defined User Personas, it is possible to customize members' experience in the community to best fit their individual preferences and needs. This may include creating specific content, events, or community features that respond to each type of user.

Guide the development of products and services: User Personas provide valuable information that can guide the development of products and services within the community. By understanding members' needs and wants, solutions can be created that effectively address their problems and add real value to their lives.

Example of User Persona:

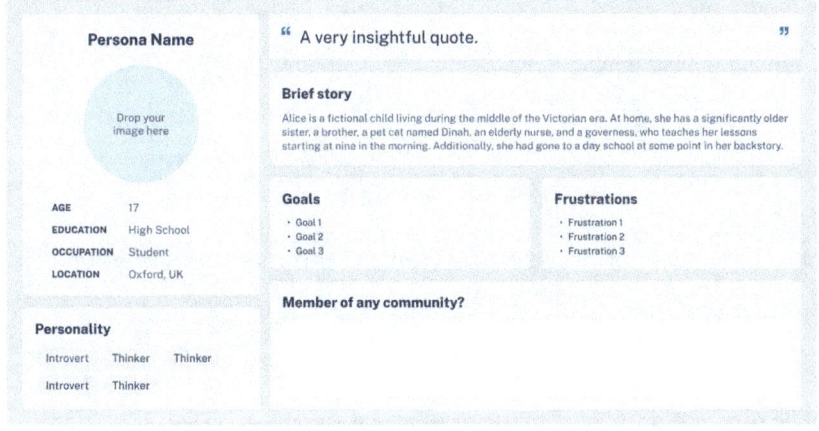

What does the Community offer its members?

Now think, what would the community give to the public? Why would anyone choose to be part of the community? What benefits would they get? A person usually joins a community influenced by the following aspects:

- Build relationships
- Contribute and help in various ways
- Share a sense of belonging and a passion
- Have a voice

Some examples of how you can reward the members of your community:

Public recognition: Highlight the most active members, on social networks, community events, or general meetings to recognize their contributions and achievements in front of the entire community.

Exclusive opportunities: Offer featured members the opportunity to participate in exclusive events, mentoring sessions, working groups or special projects that provide them with a unique and valuable experience within the community.

Tangible benefits: Provide tangible benefits, such as discounts on products or services, access to premium resources, or free memberships, as a way to reward members for their loyalty and commitment.

Personalized thank you: Send personalized thank you messages or letters of recognition to individual members, expressing your gratitude for their specific contributions and the positive impact they have had on the community.

How to involve Community members

Depending on the type of community you build, you can take action to keep its members interested and active. Some of them are:

- Gamification and rewards
- Generate conversation
- Highlight community members for their actions
- Give community members a warm welcome
- Create collaborative projects or actions
- Keep community members informed
- Explain what they commit to by being part

One of the biggest challenges is keeping community members active and interested while recruiting new members. Also keep in mind that people's interests can change over time, so even if they remain connected to the purpose and values, generate different activities and, above all, ask your community for feedback regularly to understand their level of involvement so you can transform your strategy if necessary.

Ambassadors

Designating ambassadors is a very nice way to involve the members of your community. It rewards the most passionate, active, and contributing members with a role or a badge that makes them stand out. It empowers these faithful members to be protagonists and collaborate to promote the community and transmit its message.

Maintain member loyalty

Here I describe some ways in which loyalty to a community can manifest itself:

Active participation: A person loyal to a community actively participates in its activities, events, and projects. She is willing to contribute her time, energy, and resources for the collective benefit.

Mutual support: Loyalty to a community involves supporting and supporting other members in times of need. This may include offering practical help, providing emotional support, or advocating for community interests when necessary.

Promotion and defense: People loyal to a community act as defenders and promoters of its values and causes. They are willing to speak on behalf of the community, defend its interests, and promote its vision to others.

Identification and belonging: Loyalty to a community is reflected in a deep sense of identification and belonging. Individuals feel an integral part of the community and are proud to be part of it.

Respect and commitment: Loyal people show deep respect for other members of the community, as well as its norms and values. They are committed to the well-being and continued success of the community.

Perseverance: Even in challenging times, people loyal to a community remain steadfast in their commitment and do not easily abandon their ties to it.

Incorporation of new members: Onboarding

"Onboarding" a community refers to the process of incorporating new members in an effective and welcoming way. Similar to the term used in the workplace to refer to the integration of new employees, "onboarding" in a community involves providing new members with the **information, resources, and guidance** necessary to make them feel welcome, understood, and enabled to actively participate.

During this process, it is important to provide new members with a complete understanding of the community. This includes explaining their purpose, values, standards of conduct, organizational structure, and the resources available to them, such as forums, chat groups, and shared documents.

Additionally, new members must become familiar with the community's tools and platforms. Therefore, they should be offered **guidance** on how to use these tools effectively.
It is also beneficial to introduce key community members, such as leaders, moderators, or mentors, who can offer additional guidance and support.

It is important to set **clear expectations** for new members regarding their participation, contribution, and behavior, as well as inform them about what they can expect in return.
Finally, regular follow-up and ongoing support are essential to ensure that new members are onboarded properly and to address any questions or concerns they may have throughout the onboarding process.

A powerful tool: Onboarding Journey Map

An Onboarding Journey Map is a visual representation of a person's experience with an organization during onboarding. The map will describe **important moments, points of interaction with the person, emotions, and weak points** during the journey.

It is an artifact that you can generate at the beginning and that you can improve as users join. You will learn about their behavior and experience during the onboarding journey. Make sure you take your target audience as a reference, and that the tour takes into account all the important touchpoints, such as:

- Entries from a website or social networks
- Subscription or registration forms
- Welcome emails
- Slack Invitations
- Product tours
- Others

Onboarding Journey Map example:

Onboarding phases, here:

AWARENESS → CONSIDERATION → CONVERSION → RETENTION → ADVOCACY

POSITIVE EXPERIENCE

- (+) Discovers the community
- (+) Does Research
- (+) Visits the website
- (+) Fills form registration
- (+) Joins the community

Contact points, here

NEGATIVE EXPERIENCE

- (−) Slack experience
- (−) How do I contribute?

In this area, the route has points of improvement in communication and expectations setting.

The team behind (and in front) of the Community

Many times, the idea comes from an individual, but believe me, you will need help maintaining a community. It seems like a simple task, but you must have control over several things at the same time, from onboarding new members and responding to messages on social networks to more administrative tasks.

I recommend that you associate with people who share the values you want to transmit in your community, committed people who like teamwork. Many times, decisions must be made between several people, which is why I also advise you to put together an organizational structure that establishes those responsible for different work verticals or tasks. This will help speed up decision-making and direct responsibilities.

Some of the areas over which you must have control:

Branding

Onboarding of new users

Reply messages

Member withdrawal

Stakeholders management

Coordination of tasks with the team

Metrics monitoring

Partnering with a team when building a community is essential for several reasons:

Distribution of tasks: Creating and managing a community can be overwhelming for a single person. By partnering with a team, responsibilities can be distributed more effectively, allowing a variety of tasks to be tackled, from event planning to communicating with members.

Diversity of skills and perspectives: A diverse team brings with it a wide range of skills, experiences, and perspectives. This enriches the decision-making process and creativity in the community, as different people can contribute unique ideas and innovative solutions to the challenges facing the community.

Emotional support and motivation: Working as a team provides a system of emotional support and mutual motivation. When team members share a common vision and support each other, they are more likely to remain engaged and enthusiastic over time, even when difficulties arise.

Greater reach and connection: By partnering with a team, the community can reach more people and make stronger connections with a variety of individuals and groups. Each team member can have a network of contacts that can contribute to the growth and diversity of the community.

Representation and legitimacy: A well-structured team can provide a more complete and legitimate representation of the community as a whole. This can be especially important when interacting with external entities, such as government organizations, local businesses, or media outlets.

Identify stakeholders

First, let's define a stakeholder. A stakeholder is any party interested in and impacted by the actions, decisions, and circumstances of a venture; they are also called "Stakeholders." For a company, for example, its stakeholders could be its customers, employees, shareholders, suppliers, competitors, communities, and the government.

It is essential to be clear about whom the interested parties are in your community, and for that, there is an extremely useful tool for mapping these actors: the Stakeholder Map.

The stakeholders can be:

- Internal
- External
- Primary
- Secondary
- Direct
- Indirect

Is it useful to make alliances with other communities?

Of course! It is very beneficial. It happens a lot in technology communities, for example, where a collaborative network is generated that creates synergy, either to share content or to collaborate on activities. Collaborating with similar communities is beneficial, as it can grow your audience, and you can expand horizons and possibilities. These allied communities are also within the group of stakeholders.

One way to visualize these interest groups is to create a Stakeholder Map.

This is an invaluable tool for communities for several reasons:

Identification of key stakeholders: The Stakeholder Map allows you to identify all relevant stakeholders for the community, both internal and external. This includes community members, local leaders, nonprofit organizations, local businesses, educational institutions, government officials, and other groups that may have an interest in community issues.

Understanding needs and expectations: By mapping stakeholders, the community can better understand their needs, expectations, interests, and concerns. This provides valuable information to design programs, projects, and activities that are relevant and meaningful to stakeholders.

Improved communication and collaboration: With a clear Stakeholder Map, the community can develop more effective communication and collaboration strategies. This may involve creating specific communication channels, organizing regular meetings with key stakeholders, or collaborating on joint projects to address common problems.

Relationship Management: Facilitates relationship management with different stakeholders by providing an overview of who they are, what their interests are, and how they can influence the community. This allows efforts and resources to be prioritized to maintain positive and constructive relationships with those who have a significant impact.

Decision-making support: By better understanding the perspectives and needs of key stakeholders, the Stakeholder Map can guide community decision-making. This helps ensure that decisions are inclusive and transparent, and considers potential impacts on all stakeholders involved.

Identify the right platform

When choosing the platform for your community, it is essential to consider several aspects to ensure that it meets our needs and those of our members. First, we need to deeply **understand** what our community is looking for in terms of interaction and functionality. This involves determining if we need functions such as real-time chat, discussion forums, or the ability to share multimedia content, among others.

Additionally, it is essential to evaluate the platform's **accessibility and usability**. We need to ensure that it is easy to use for all members, regardless of their technical skill level, and that it offers a seamless user experience on mobile and desktop devices.

Another crucial aspect is the **platform's security and privacy**. To protect our members' information, we should look for a platform that offers robust security measures, such as data encryption and configurable privacy options.

Considering the costs associated with the platform is also important. Evaluate if the cost fits our budget and if the platform offers good value for the money invested. Some platforms are free, while others require a subscription with additional premium features.

Additionally, we must investigate the platform's **scalability**. As our community grows, we need to ensure that the platform can handle an increase in traffic and users without compromising performance.

Exploring **customization** options can also be beneficial. Some platforms offer options to tailor the appearance and functionality to our specific needs, which can help create a unique experience for our members.

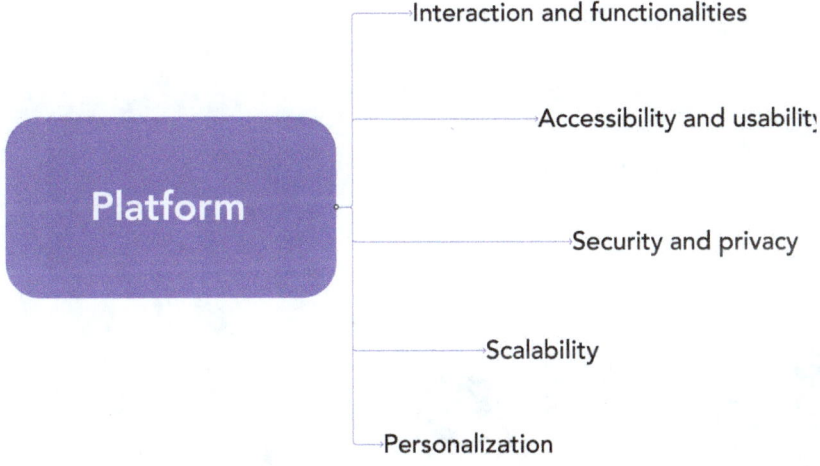

"Community is much more than belonging to something; It's about doing something together that makes belonging matter."

Brian Solis

IV. The Future

Planning is key

Planning is something that will order your community and your mind. You will plan activities for the week, for the month, and you will also plan for the long-term future. Before I mentioned the concept of vision, that will be your north star to move forward. Your community should identify with that north, for as long as it is active, and if for some reason you imagine a different future, that's okay, and the vision will change.

Whatever the case, always keep in mind to look toward the future and grow toward that place and that ideal that the community wants to achieve.

A community can plan in different periods:
- Weekly
- Monthly
- Quarterly
- Annual
- Bi-annual
- + 2 years

It is healthy for a community for its team to connect regularly, not only to stay aligned on tasks but to check the level of commitment of each team member and whether people remain aligned with the purpose. For example, once or twice a year you can do a retrospective exercise and a team alignment meeting, but the cadence will be defined by each team. Setting milestones with the team is a way to grow and measure growth.

Some useful tools to get organized:

Kanban
Agile project management tool designed to visualize work, limit work in progress, and maximize efficiency.

Roadmap
Visual representation of key goals and milestones in the development of a project, which helps guide the process and communicate strategic direction to all interested parties.

Gantt Diagram
Graphic tool whose objective is to show the expected dedication time for different tasks or activities over a given total time.

Decision Matrix
It helps to identify options and compare the alternatives, and make decisions based on the evaluation of criteria.

Mental Maps
It is a graphic organizer, where the main idea is defined in the center, and from there branches of other ideas emerge.

Stakeholder Map
This tool, although it is not planning in itself, is very useful. Describe all the people who may be impacted, or impact your community.

How do you maintain a Community? Does it "end" at some point?

The community will exist, as long as there is the will of both its leaders and its members to continue being part, and as long as there continues to be a reason for its existence.

A community needs to stay active to survive and grow. This aspect comes hand in hand with seeking feedback and planning. Plan short- and medium-term activities to stay one step ahead and be able to focus on the value you continue to deliver to people.

> People like to belong to a place that inspires and empowers them, so as long as your community offers that, they will be safe, but it's not everything.

Don't lose sight of the data!

Analyze participation and behavior metrics. What initiatives does the community prefer? What content generates the most sharing? Having this information will allow you to **refine the strategy to focus on what works.**

Consider that the community may cease to exist at some point, or that you can transfer it or even sell it. An established and successful community is a very valuable asset, and it is common that over the years, its leaders change or the community becomes something new. Also, accept that a community may need to come to an end, so design an "exit plan" for its members and communicate on the relevant channels. Always try to innovate and never lose authenticity.

Metrics to measure Community growth

Number of active members: Monitor the number of members who regularly participate in the community, whether by contributing posts, comments, or participating in events and activities.

Member Retention Rate: Calculates the percentage of members who continue to participate in the community over a given period, indicating long-term retention and engagement.

New Members: Tracks the number of new members joining the community in a given period, indicating the growth and attraction of new participants.

Participation in events and activities: Evaluate participation in community events and activities, such as meetings, workshops, webinars, or social events, to measure interest and active participation.

Online Interactions and Engagement: Analyzes online interactions, such as posts, comments, likes, and shares on social media platforms or forums, to measure online engagement and participation.

Feedback and member satisfaction: Collect feedback regularly through surveys, or interviews to evaluate member satisfaction and gather ideas to improve the community.

Impact and Results: Evaluate the impact of the community on members, such as professional development, connections made, collaborative projects, or any other measurable results.

Reach and visibility: Analyze metrics such as post reach, number of followers, or search engine visibility to evaluate the visibility and spread of the community.

By monitoring and analyzing these metrics regularly, you will be able to better understand community performance, identify areas for improvement, and take action to drive growth and continued member engagement.

"The greatness of a community is most accurately measured by the compassionate actions of its members."

Coretta Scott king

V. Case Study: Mujeres IT

Mujeres IT

I told you at the beginning of this book that I am the founder of Mujeres IT. A community that celebrated 6 years of existence in 2023 and currently brings together more than 1,000 women in technology in Latin America and the world. I will tell you how this community was born and has managed to take off and maintain itself with a growing number of members and followers.

As a technology student, I observed the low proportion of women in the field from an early age, and I was able to observe it even more when I started working in technology companies. I wondered why there were so few women in the field; I wanted to meet them and bring them together. From this concern, the idea and concept of IT Women arose: a space that brings together IT women and makes their talent visible.
Then I got to work. With my resources, I began to build a blog, a web directory with profiles of women who worked in the area.

I was in charge of generating communication and disseminating the project among my contacts, and I was surprised by women's great interest in participating. I had proven my hypothesis, the world needed a place like this.

After a few months, there were already about 300 women on that blog, which we later called "Directory," and I thought it was time to stop and consider how to carry the project forward in a sustainable and scalable way since its growth was evident.
At a networking event, I met who today is one of the community leaders, Victo-

ria Perez. At that time, I told her about the project. She immediately wanted to participate and collaborate in the organization, so there were already two of us on the team, and the efforts were divided.

Then, the third leader joined, and more volunteers who believed in our mission joined, and the community began to grow, but so did the responsibilities.
To this day, the strongest bond that unites us as an organizing team and as a community is our passion for our mission: wanting to build a network of women to sustain us and make us visible.

Women want to occupy spaces in the tech world because we maintain that there is a gender gap in the area and that the lack of diversity in technology has severe consequences for the entire society.

We have set goals that mean growth for the community.
The history of Mujeres IT in milestones:

- When we turned one year old, we held a face-to-face meeting in which we met our community face to face.
- We launch the official website of Mujeres IT
- We launched our first mentoring program
- We created the official Slack of IT Women
- We reached 4000 followers on Instagram
- The Board of Directors reaches its first 1,000 members
- We held MITConf, our first online technology and gender conference

Setting milestones helps us measure the success of our community and visualize future goals.

Communication strategy, our tone of voice

The team was always aligned that our tone of voice would be informal and approachable. We wanted to be a friendly community so that whoever is part of it could find a woman to talk to face to face, and without intermediaries. The founders also offer direct contact with members of the community. This is one of our differentiators, and to this day it continues to be something that the members value, immediacy in communication.

Communication channels and platforms

We defined that we would communicate mainly through microblogging on Instagram, a format that we like for its immediacy with the audience. We also chose Slack as the exclusive means of interaction with Board members. This medium allows us to segment members to generate better-targeted communications and conversations in context, in addition to allowing the exchange of digital material.

For our more formal profile, we decided to host communications to organizations on LinkedIn.
We have a third communication channel which is the Newsletter, and it is exclusive for women who are part of the Mujeres IT Directory.

What value does Mujeres IT deliver to its members?

Whoever joins the community has benefits. In addition to being part of a huge network of women, they can connect with opportunities and potentially develop their professional skills, they are given access to Slack, receive a Newsletter with exclusive information, and have access to benefits specially created for IT Women.

The women in the community may also be featured, tell their stories and experiences to the world, or speak at tech events.

What value do they deliver to the community?

This is something we have worked hard on, how to communicate the commitment assumed by those who make up the community. Because it is natural to assume that a financial contribution must be made, or that it must be compensated in some way. We continue to work with the team on how to report back to the community, and to be as transparent as possible. What we ask in return when joining Mujeres IT is that each woman can commit to helping another.

Data is a very valuable asset for Mujeres IT. Thanks to the data that members provide at the time of registration, we are able to map the reality of women in IT, both in demographic terms and in terms of roles held in the industry.

Looking to the future

We are six years old, and the community has reached its maturity level. It is time to rethink ourselves. After six years of sustained growth and with a list of milestones achieved, we had to rethink our commitment to the cause for which we exist and the commitment of each of us who are part of a volunteer team. Creating close ties between team members is vital to speaking honestly about our commitment. At Mujeres IT we work together, but we are also friends, and that closeness that we propose on the inside, we also reflect on the outside.

Mujeres IT wants to continue functioning, and transforming, but never losing sight of its objectives and always connecting and vibrating through that bond, which is our mission.

VI. Checklist

A reference list to create your community

Checklist

- [ ] **Reflect on your community's purpose in the world**
  Analyze well the present moment, the context and the future.

- [ ] **Define the Mission**
  It should be brief, memorable and easy to understand, but at the same time, it should reflect the essence of the organization and its long-term vision.

- [ ] **Define the Vision**
  An effective vision should be clear, specific, achievable, relevant and meaningful, and describe the desired state in the future.

- [ ] **Define the profile of the followers**
  Value Proposition Canvas and User Persona.

- [ ] **Think about what the community offers its members**
  Why would anyone choose to be part of the community? What benefits would you get?

- [ ] **Think about how to involve community members**
  What methods and strategies I will use to keep members active.

- [ ] **Onboarding design**
  Onboarding Journey Map

- [ ] **Build a team**
  Integrate people who have the same interests and who enjoy teamwork.

- [ ] **Identify stakeholders**
  Stakeholder Map

- [ ] **Define a planning process**
  Consider which tools are right for your team.

VII. Community Planner

Registration of the creation of my community

Community name:

This is the purpose of my community in the world.
I make an analysis of the present moment, the context and the future:

This is the mission of my community:
Remember: It should be brief, memorable and easy to understand, but at the same time, it should reflect the essence of the or- ganization and its long-term vision.

This is the vision of my community:
Remember: An effective vision should be clear, specific, achievable, relevant and meaningful, and describe the desired state in the future.

This is the profile of the audience:
Remember: You can use Value Proposition Canvas and User Persona.
Describe the needs, wants, and motivations of your audience.

Persona 1

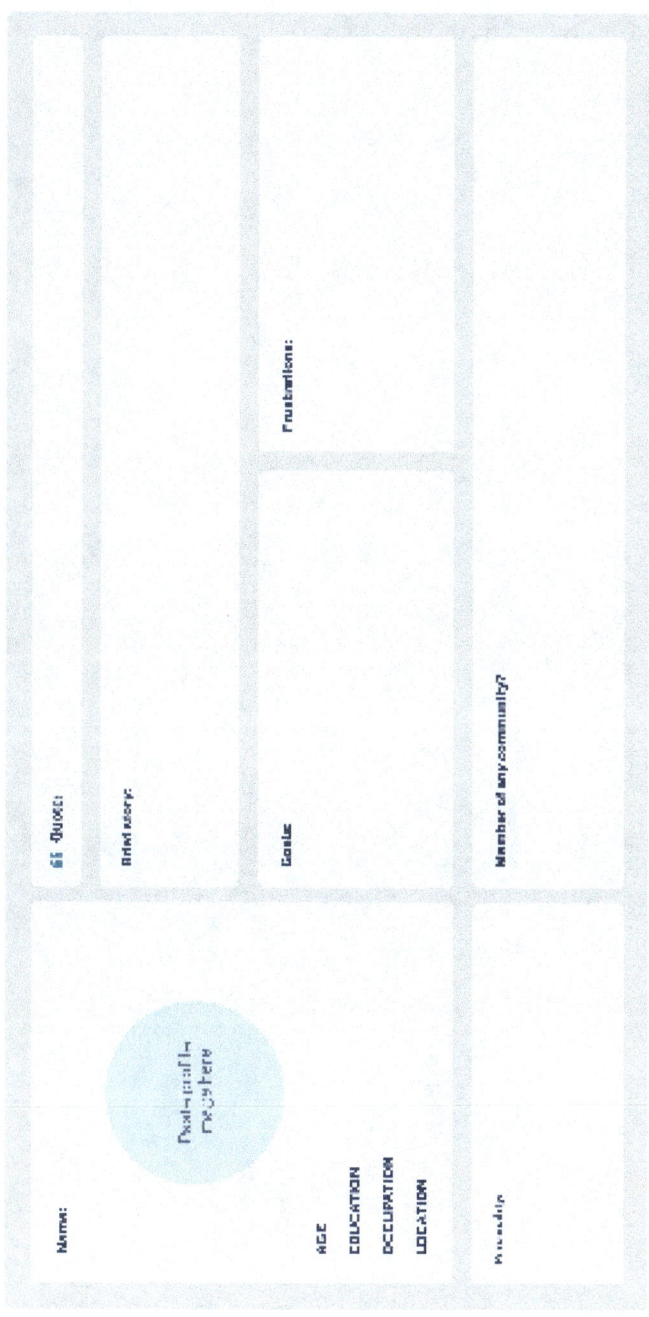

Persona 2

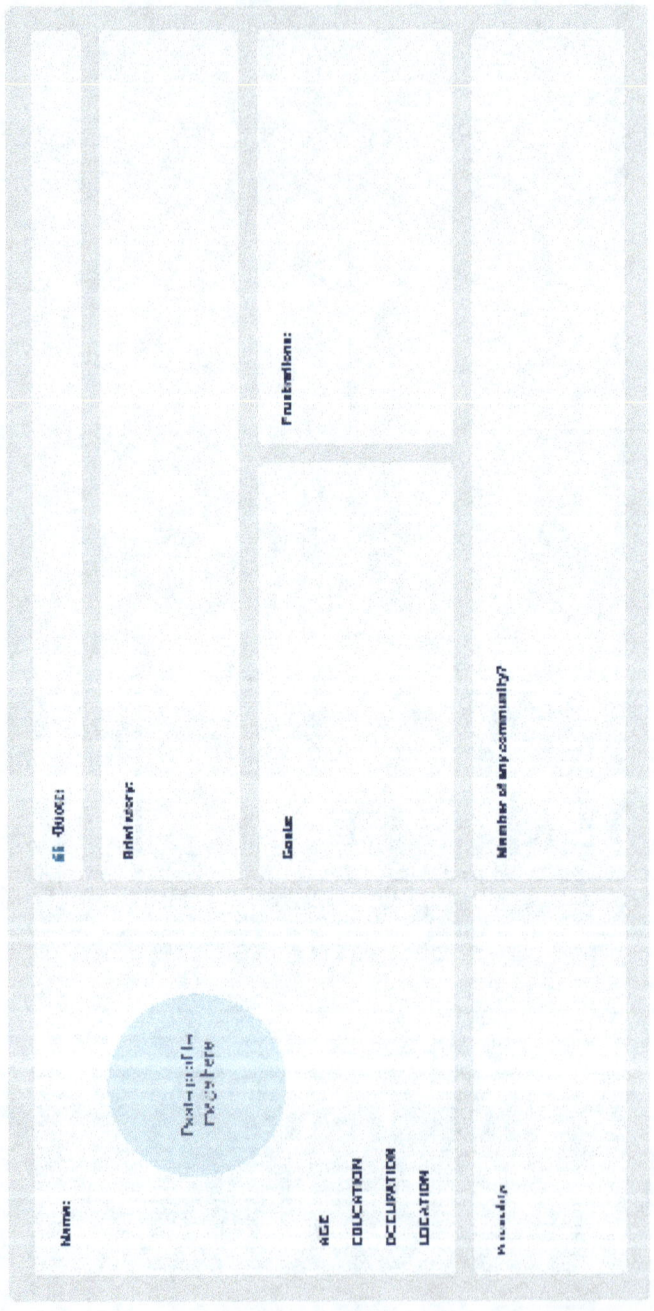

This is what the community offers its members:
Why would anyone choose to be part of the community?

This is how I will involve community members:
What methods and strategies I will use to keep members active?

Stakeholder Map:

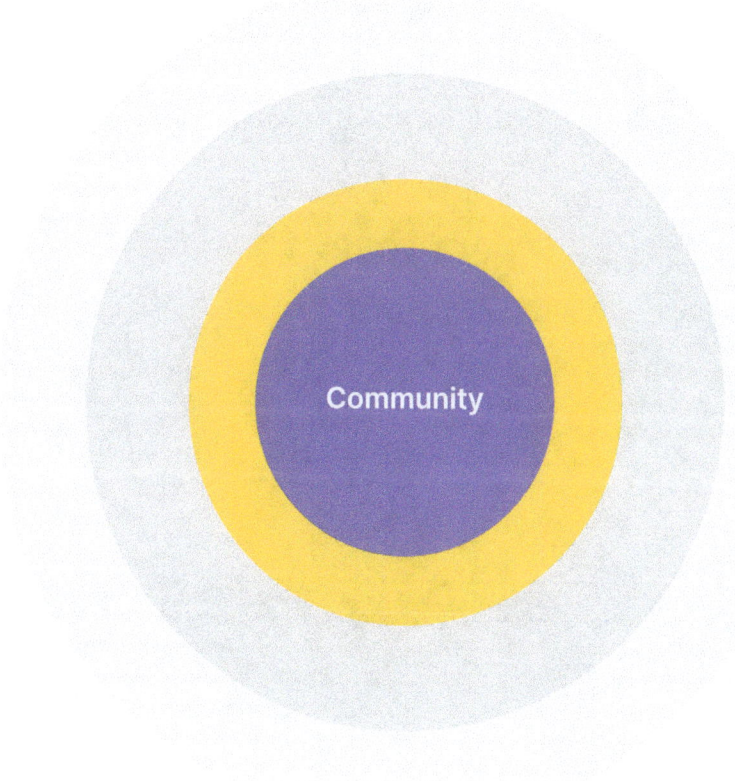

Onboarding Journey Map:

My "planning the future" process:

Planning tools:

Ceremonies:

Backlog of long-term ideas :

Backlog of long-term ideas :

Credits

Illustrations:
www.freepik.es
https://www.freepik.es/autor/pikisuperstar

Value Proposition Canvas official template
https://www.strategyzer.com/library/the-value-proposition-canvas

User Persona template:
https://www.figma.com/file/eeA4h0U0ViSre9nUJA1iS9/User-Persona-%26-Empathy-Map-(Community)?type=design&node-id=0-1&mode=-design&t=jugTmAAuPwqTBO9Z-0

© 2024 Lucia Bustamante
All rights reserved.

www.luciabustamante.com

www.ingramcontent.com/pod-product-compliance
Lightning Source LLC
Chambersburg PA
CBHW070200230526
45471CB00002B/742